YOU CAN
QUOTE ME
ON THIS

WORDS TO EMPOWER YOU AND AWAKEN YOUR CONSCIOUSNESS

ELSA MENDOZA, CCC

ISBN-10: 1547180986
ISBN-13: 978-1547180981

*I lovingly dedicate this book to you,
the reader.*

INTRODUCTION

Throughout the millennia, quotes have been used at the beginning or end of a speech, or during a conversation. They can also be seen on signs, billboards, restaurant table napkins and menus, business giveaways, greeting cards, novelty items or simply compiled in a book. Philosophers, teachers, thinkers, tycoons and many others have used quotes to express their observations, life experiences, their joy and their pain. I use them in the same manner these philosophers, teachers, and thinkers did. But most importantly, I use them to inspire, motivate, uplift and empower myself, as well as to challenge my thinking and change my perspectives. This book was written with the goal for you to have that same experience, specifically to raise self-awareness and empowerment, experience hope and change the way you think. I have written hundreds of quotes during my spiritual journey and these were handpicked especially for you. Your interpretation of these quotes might be different than mine due to your life experiences and level of awareness, but the end goal is the same. There is a backstory and insight to each quote so you can further understand and address your curiosities on why each of these was written. The book is divided into six chapters. You can read from the beginning or go directly to the specific chapter you prefer. Whichever you choose will lead you to the same goal of self-awareness and empowerment and a completely different mindset.

Peace, blessings, and love,
Elsa

TABLE OF CONTENTS

YOU CAN QUOTE ME ON THIS

CHAPTER ONE

Quotes to Self

1.

"You are love-d."

You are LOVE. You came from a Creator of love, created by and out of love, to love and be loved. Everything exists because of love. You are nothing and no one else but this. Without love, there is no life. In times of melancholy, this is a good reminder to inspire you to live and do everything out of love.

2.

"You are not your name, your body, your work title, your religion and your things. You are the greatest peace, joy and the grandest love."

In this physical world that we live in, we've been influenced to believe that we are what we have achieved and acquired. We have been limited by these beliefs that have caused us to forget that we are beyond this. I have experienced a sort of comfort by being financially, materially and emotionally (by having someone) stable. I belong to the society and life is just beautiful, I said. But why was I still yearning for something, even if I knew that I already have what a person could desire? Until I realized that my soul was already nudging me and telling me that I was forgetting my true nature, which is the same as God's. And this is joy, peace, and love. My satisfaction and contentment cannot be measured by my acquisitions nor be dependent on them. I started to question myself, my purpose, my true happiness and the Universe itself. And then I found my answers, and my spiritual journey began. I immersed myself in nonstop reading, listening, attending discussions on self-awareness and continuously searching for answers. I got in touch with my true being. I am beyond my ego which is constantly hungry to be noticed and to be satisfied by more acquisitions. I discovered that I am a spiritual being just having a human experience. I am consciousness, energy, and a vibrational being. I was born rich and most of all, born out of love.

3.

"Know your self well and then create and live it."

I have lived without really paying attention to myself, to my soul specifically. I did not make much quiet time or "me" time as they call it. I just went on with my life. What I knew back then was that I survived each day by working hard, getting paid, enjoying the fruits of my labor, and having someone to love. I thought that all of these were life itself. Until I got sick and tired of the endless and mundane routine. I sought for something more meaningful than this. I took some time off and surrounded myself with spiritual authors, philosophers, influencers, movers and shakers of our world—people working for the good of humanity. I learned that I am a co-creator to our

Creator whom we call God. A Goddess, given a free will to create the life I desire to have. I started creating and reinventing myself. Now I'm an author empowering you. WOW! I am consciousness and the Universe itself. The stuff that makes up the stars is the same stuff that I have in me! And so my life is no longer routine.

4.

"Everything about you is beautiful. Believe, know and remember this."

Didn't I just say, the stuff that made up the stars is the same stuff we're made up of? It's not hearsay or a theory. There's a scientific explanation to all of this and the facts to back it up. Sentient beings are made up of carbon, oxygen, calcium, and iron. Sound familiar? These are elements found in the periodic table, elements that also make up the stars. I always knew we were created in the image and likeness of God, but now it was also backed by science. And this inspired me to write this quote in full conviction that we are beyond our physical forms. So when someone tells me that I am beautiful, I just reply, "I know, so are you, thank you."

5.

"I only have two choices in life - be happy or be miserable."

For years I have used these words to serve as my own reminder that I always have a choice in life whenever I find myself in a state of sadness. It helps me to get back on my feet and move on with my life.

6.

"Your own feelings and intuition are your best guide and friend. Feel it, listen to it, and thank it, as your soul speaks through it."

I consider our intuition and feelings to be gifts. They came along with our inner being to help and guide us. They help me in my decision-making process, whether the decisions are big or little. There were times that I did not listen and made the wrong decisions resulting in an unpleasant turn of events in my life. In the past, I have involved myself with someone and stayed in the relationship despite the negative feelings I felt while my gut was telling me not to. The relationship did not end well, and it was a very traumatic experience for me. Trusting my intuition helps me recognize the people who are sincere, true, and loyal to me.

7.

"Don't take things too personally, it's not always about you."

I wrote this quote because of the endless drama I have created in my life before and the drama that I also see and feel everywhere. I have learned that this is a waste of energy and only adds to my difficulties in life. It hinders me from growing. I realized I made things complicated. Life is supposed to be enjoyed rather than be consumed by dramas. There are things that you just have to let go. Nowadays, you see these a lot on social media. I have witnessed people attacking each other by exchanging angry words and posts, feeling that they have been personally attacked by others. We can learn to just let go and not take everything personally as not all posts, quotes, movies, or articles are intentionally directed at us.

8.

"In our lowest moments, we find our true powerful self."

This quote came about when I recalled my past experiences during childhood. The environment I grew up in was a violent one, filled with physical and verbal abuse by my family as a form of discipline. Because of this foundation, I strived to be successful in my career and become stable, independent, and strong. I faced and handled this the best I could. I forgave my parents and siblings who have been difficult with me. I found the power in my lowest times through forgiveness.

9.

"No need to impress, no need to compete, we are all the same and we come from the same source. Everyone is special."

The lack of self-confidence and knowledge of our true nature and higher selves in this ego driven society results in people succumbing to the need to: impress others; fill up emptiness, and feel acknowledged and important. The need to show off and to be right has always been the number one reason there are still endless disagreements and even wars on our entire planet. We can start to believe that we are one, we are all special and that our source is love. Soon, our planet and society will be in a much better state.

10.

"Why seek approval when you have already been approved to 'be' by the Creator of the Universe?"

Some people go to the extent of changing or enhancing their physical appearance just to belong, to be understood, and to be accepted by others. They are forgetting their true worth, their true nature, and their power. There's no need to seek the approval of others. Acceptance comes from yourself first.

11.

"When someone wishes you well, receive it with gladness. When someone is trying to avoid you, still wish them well, move on, and do not disturb them anymore."

This quote came about after I experienced being avoided or just ignored by friends and even family. My ego's reaction was to retaliate at first, but instead of being affected by this, I learned to let go, move on, and keep my joy. I continue to wish them well as I am aware that what they are going through is really about them and has nothing to do with me. Their issue is something that I know nothing about. I just keep my distance, respect their space, and try not to take it personally. As I practice this, it becomes a habit then my life becomes much easier and happier.

12.

"Slow down.
Pay attention. You might
miss living your life."

Yes, learn to pause. I got sick before from working too much and wanting to get everything done right away. I forgot to live in the present moment. I did not give myself the chance to appreciate the beauty of a day. This quote serves as a reminder to myself whenever I catch myself being consumed or stressed about things that do not require my immediate attention. So, slow down, my friend.

13.

"Mind your own business. Focus only on your life. Do not stick your nose in other people's paths. And do not compare your life to others. See how your life improves."

It has been my observation that some people are just nosy. They compare their lives and the way they live and do things to others. I got inspired to write this because of my actual experiences with people I know. People normally engage in comparison because of their need to identify who is better and their desire to live the life that others have. We can improve our lives when we focus on our own and realize that every person has his own unique path. Life requires no comparison at all.

14.

"The best relationship that you can have is with yourself. Be the one that you can really trust, depend on, and always tell yourself the truth."

The people we meet will have different influences and impacts on our lives. In the process of building relationships with people, we either experience joy or pain. People also come and go in our lives, and we are sometimes left with just ourselves. Through all the life challenges and glorious experiences, there is only one constant participant, ourselves. Wherever we go, we are but with ourselves. Earlier in my life, regardless of feelings and emotions, there was only one way in which I rewarded myself . . . to fill my life with material things. I have learned in my spiritual journey that I am more than my physical self, my achievements, my acquisitions and the identity I created for myself. I am a spiritual being and a co-creator, a Goddess made from love, to love . . . the highest form of creation. I have the power to change any situation by simply changing my mindset. Having realized these things, I now have a better relationship with myself and with others. I live a healthier lifestyle. I have come to accept and appreciate more of myself and have been more sensitive to my intuition. I love myself as I am.

15.

"Just let it go and let it flow for you to grow."

I detested the countless hospital visits where they had to draw blood samples from me due to Aplastic Anemia, but I went along with the process. Some days were acceptable and some days were not. There were times that I did not want to show up. In spite of all this, I realized that for me to experience healing, I had to cooperate and participate in the process. After almost four years, the day came when the doctor released me and told me that I was finally okay. Had I been so stubborn about this, I would not be here to share my story with you. Had I not cooperated in the process, I would not be able to enjoy the healing from God. Had I not participated, I would not

have learned the valuable lessons my illness taught
me.

16.

"If you really like, want, wish, hope, desire and are interested in something and someone, you always find a way."

I was inspired to write this during the time I was organizing a meet-up with friends. It was weeks ahead of planning and everyone agreed and confirmed that they were available on the schedule. Everyone was excited. However, it did not materialize in the end. One person had to cancel because of a last minute appointment and the rest suddenly had other reasons not to attend. I felt that I was the only one with the real "want" at this moment. The meet-up would have still materialized had everyone "wanted" it. The only thing I am saying here is when there's a real want, a desire, you will find a way to make it happen! So, what do you desire right now?

17.

"Personal life experiences are great teachers and more effective than gained knowledge alone."

My life experiences taught me a lot and have allowed me to create something meaningful, like this book. My experiences have given me an outlet to share what I've learned with you. I fully believe that you will too. We may have learned from school, and what we've believed and followed in books we've read. But what about your actual and real experiences without any influence from people or literature? Knowledge is nothing without the actual experience.

18.

"You always have a choice and you always have time. Stop telling yourself that you don't."

When I was in my early 20's, I thought that I did not have much choice and time to improve my life. But it turned out that I did because I made a decision to. If I had stayed in the stressful and rough environment that I grew up in, I would not have grown and would not be able to share this book with you. Had I chosen to believe that I had no hope in getting well when I was sick, I might have already died. Had I not left an ugly relationship, I would have lived a life of regret. Had I chosen not to change my thinking, I would have continued living a life of misery.

19.

"You cannot impose your beliefs on people and force them to believe, but you can motivate, encourage and empower them to be the best that they can be."

One sunny day, I was picked up at lunch from work by a lady I met through a friend and the head of youth ministry of a Christian church. Off we went to a quiet complex near the park. There I was asked to decide to join their church and receive Jesus Christ as my Lord and Savior. There was pressure applied and she told me that if I didn't decide at that very moment, hell awaited and that she wouldn't leave until I gave her my decision. I found myself in a difficult situation that time, but I had the courage to say no. I felt so relieved by that decision. As an attendee of another Christian church at the time and once a religious person, I fully understood how my church or religion operated. I am aware of the exuberance of each attendee to evangelize or recruit someone because of the belief that Jesus Christ will save them from their sins and that they belong to and found the right church. However, as religion teaches about love, it should then be patient, respecting of people's beliefs, unifying, and most of all not imposing.

20.

"Not all will like, accept, and love you. And you will not like, accept, and love all."

Each one of us is a vibrational being emitting frequencies. Like attracts like. Your vibe attracts your tribe. Whoever you are with right now is whom you have attracted. The rest who are out of your circle or your tribe are simply not on the same frequency as you are, and this is just normal and nothing to be worried about or take personally. We have the right to choose the people we like to surround ourselves with, people who will support, and celebrate with us.

21.

"In silence, I clearly heard all there was to know about myself."

I learned to appreciate the present moment. I am a spiritual and physical being who is beautiful and I am love-d.

22.

"There's always a nice way of saying things."

I remember a verse in the Bible (Matthew 12:34) that goes like this: out of the abundance of the heart the mouth speaks. I have experienced having a few co-workers who, every time they open their mouths, only negative stories or comments come out. This affected the work atmosphere and everyone's mood. No wonder these former co-workers of mine have never ending problems in their respective families and relationships. I too had my share of delivering bad news or simply just whining until I noticed that it was taking a toll on my health. It takes practice and discipline to think and choose what you are about to say. Consider the effects. Ask yourself, will this be encouraging, uplifting, or just the opposite?

23.

"Just be who you want to be. It's your own decision and voice that matters, not other's."

I, being the youngest in the family, had a choice to stay and live with them. The strictness, physical and verbal abuse of my parents and bullying by my siblings, made me decide to leave. They tried to persuade me to stay but I was firm in my decision to be independent and to have a peaceful life. I even took it a step further and left the country. I just wanted to be far away from all the toxicity. Looking back, I can pat myself on the back for having done this. The painful experience inspired and motivated me to do better and be the person I am today. Everyone is different in handling situations like this. Once you have decided, the Universe will show you resources you have never thought about. Know that nothing is impossible. You will be guided, supported, and helped by the Divine intelligence and power that we call God.

24.

"You are never a victim unless you think you are."

Everything starts with our thoughts. Anything that is repeatedly thought about and processed becomes a belief, which eventually develops into a corresponding behavior. I could not forget the woman in the news a few years ago whose son was killed and she eventually forgave his killer. She even treated him as her own son too in the end. This is the power of our true self. The woman did not think that she was a victim but rather showed what love is—that it's boundless and limitless, and non-judgmental. I would have chosen to think and to act like a victim too from the physical and verbal abuse I received from my parents, but instead, I turned things around to become a much better person by forgiving them.

25.

"Self-forgiveness and self-acceptance are things that you can do, create, enjoy, and gift yourself without regrets."

When I found and experienced the power of forgiveness for my family, I also applied it to myself. I was able to quickly move on with my life and change my perspective of things too. Now, I have learned to accept and appreciate myself more, and the manifestation of this in my life is peace, gratitude, and love. This is a priceless gift I have given myself. You can try it too. Allow yourself.

26.

"When there is lack and sadness, there is a disconnection from God. Recharge your connection and power before anything else."

First things first, all things living and non-living have a source. For our smartphones to be able to function well and serve their purpose, they have to be charged to the source. The same principle applies to us humans. Whenever we feel at a loss, we go back to God for wisdom and strength. We connect to recharge and get revitalized so we can create ourselves anew.

27.

"It's not that difficult to love and accept people. I started with myself first."

I believe that one way to understand people further and stop passing judgment is to know yourself first. Having a better understanding and acceptance of yourself leads to the same understanding and acceptance of others, as we all come from the same source, live on the same planet, breathe the same oxygen, and have the same physical composition. No one is more entitled than the other. Everyone is special.

CHAPTER TWO

Quotes for People

28.

"We are constantly evolving creatures; therefore, we are not really getting older, we are just getting newer."

One of the reasons I wrote this is because of my desire to share the healing that took place in my life. In 2008, I was diagnosed with Aplastic Anemia. I had blood transfusions and I was in and out of the hospital for almost four years until I became well and was released by the doctors. As I look back on the process and changes that took place, I realize that nothing is permanent. We live in an expanding Universe, one where evolution is present. This is our life. Nothing is permanent except change. Every second, there is someone being born and there is someone dying. Also, I have noticed through the years that as we get older, we also get wiser. Therefore, we obviously have learned and experienced more. And when we learn more, we create ourselves anew. Think about the cells in our bodies that rejuvenate. Wounds and small cuts simply heal and knit, right?

29.

"There is always something to appreciate about and learn from each other. Make it a habit of finding and seeing it. People are beautiful."

Based on my observations, people have a habit of saying negative things about other people. I have witnessed this in the news, actual conversations, and have even read it in magazines. This has become the nature of humans, and sadly the unpleasant things are usually the most talked about or trending. It is time to change this habit as it affects our faith in humanity and the power of people. We are all beautiful, and we should start the habit of appreciating each other, magnifying each other's strengths, building each other up, and complimenting each other.

30.

"People change. We can never use the same judgment on a person today that we used in the past. Judgments are merely ideas formed in the past, passed on by the judge, who himself has also changed."

As we normally hear, nothing is permanent except change. We are not the way we think, speak, and act when we were five years old. Nobody remains the same. Even our physical bodies change. This is how evolution works. It's just a continuous process like life.

31.

"Our personalities, choices, customs, traditions and beliefs may differ, but one thing that we all have in common is love. So be love."

I have traveled the world, lived in three countries and have had the chance to work with people from hundreds of different nationalities. Yes, I can say that we are all linked with each other. Have you not realized that we feel sad for others when we see them crying and happy for those we see laughing? We also feel rage and anger for those who cannot defend themselves from injustice and inequality. Our impulse is to help when someone is in need. Why is this so? This is our true nature, and it is beautiful. We are all beautiful. We are but love.

32.

"Each one of us is a product of greatness, joy, and love. Are you living it?"

This is a quote of encouragement for when I find myself doubting my ability to do greater things, even during the time I was writing this book. I questioned myself, can this help others? Can this motivate? Can this book raise awareness of people's greatness and power? Will people learn from this? What do you think?

33.

**"Do not neglect your
health while pursuing your
dreams. Success and wealth
are worth nothing on your
deathbed."**

I have been sick before because I forgot about
myself. I was too focused on work, pushed
myself to the limit, stretched myself too thin, and
became consumed by stress. I thought that just by
eating, drinking, sleeping, and getting a bit of
exercise, I would be good to go and survive. I was
so consumed by life that I forgot to pause and
listen to what my body was actually telling me.
One day, I found bruises all over my body, saw
that my lips were pale and white, I felt exhausted

and fatigued and had difficulty breathing. Next thing I know, I was inside an ambulance getting rushed to the hospital. There I was told that I was like a ticking time bomb and any moment I could have died. My blood count was so low that I passed out. For almost four years, I was in and out of the hospital for blood monitoring. Ever since that incident, I promised to take better care of myself and be more health conscious. I make it a point to surround myself with positivity and joy, and so should you.

34.

"As a person changes, so do his beliefs. This requires respect from everyone. Not judging but accepting."

Everyone is working on himself according to his level of awareness. My experiences from the past have propelled me to improve myself for the better. I started to rewire my thinking, being more spiritual rather than religious. I have experienced being mocked on this especially by some people who are close to me. To them, my changes were a joke, unacceptable, and I was misinterpreted and judged. This experience motivated me to write this quote. As we are evolving creatures, respect should be given to those who'd like to be better. Encouragement, support, and acceptance would help too instead of mockery.

35.

"NOW *is the time to express love for each other, not later, not tomorrow, and not even in the last breath."*

How many times have I heard people with regrets say: "If only I had told him that . . . if only I had shown her that . . . if only he was still alive . . ." I have lost my parents and I was not able to see both of them in their last hours. We were thousands of miles apart between Asia and the United States. Both of them were cremated two days after their passing, limiting my time to prepare and travel. I usually told them that I loved them during our long distance phone calls, and because of this, I had no feeling of regrets or guilt. At least I had the chance of sending them my love even if it was just through words. So, what are you waiting for?

36.

"When you can and if you can, be the source of unity and not of separation."

We are powerful beings contributing to the Collective Consciousness. Collective Consciousness is the common thought or belief of the majority. A single thought can change situations and people. As we are aware of the present condition of our world, are you conscious of the kind of source you are? Are you a good source that makes the world a better place? Or just the opposite? Remember, our thoughts are like magnets. If you emit positive frequencies or thoughts, you can expect positive results.

37.

"If you can allow yourself to be sad, worried, anxious and sick, you can also allow yourself to be happy, at peace, and healthy. That's how powerful you are."

This quote was inspired by my experience of being sick and then getting well. The quote is a summary of exactly what happened to me back in 2008. Each one of us has the power to change our life story. I allowed myself to change the way I think and believe, and then healing took over in no time. Remember the power of your thoughts.

38.

"Never cease to wish others well, as the same well-wishes will come back to you."

It can be difficult sometimes to wish others well, especially those with whom you've had challenges. I had my share of difficulty, but I thought to myself, what damage would wishing others well in spite of our differences, do in my life? You reap what you sow.

39.

"It will only happen when you BELIEVE."

I believed that I'd get well and be released from the hospital when I was diagnosed with Aplastic Anemia, and I did. I believed that I'd graduate from grad school despite emotional stress, and I did. I believed that I'd have a happy, peaceful and satisfying life, and I did. I believed that I'd be able to write a book that will change someone's life, and I did. Just believe, see it already happening, and feel it my friend.

40.

"Words from the very heart and highest self bring and call forth joy, truth, life, and love."

Nothing can be sweeter than honest, loving, and encouraging words, whether you hear them from someone or you say them to someone. It's free and does not require much effort. Words have a powerful effect on people. A single word can either damage or build. I have experienced being verbally abused, and it's painful, and so I am doing the opposite.

CHAPTER THREE

Quotes about God

41.

"God is who and what and why and how you think, see, feel, and believe God is. It is an individualized philosophy."

I was born and raised in a Catholic country, educated in Catholic schools from kindergarten to college. After college, I became a Christian and was actively involved in a Christian church. Long story short, being religious did not really work out for me because of the confusing information I received describing God. Some would say God is unconditionally loving but at the same time a punisher of disobedience and sin. It made it difficult for me to be partners with

God until I became a non-denominational person. After learning, discovering, and being reminded of my place in this Universe and my relationship with God, I have learned that God can only be defined according to one's experience. I do not need to belong to any religion to feel God's presence, power, and love. God is the entire Universe.

42.

"God is ALL. The good and bad, the Heaven and Hell, the beginning and end, the living and dead, the real and unreal, the love and hate, the male and female, the you and me."

It is my personal experience and belief that there is a force, Divine presence and Divine intelligence that others call God in this Universe, that supports us in the process we go through on a daily basis. In the challenges I have faced in life, I found God in my sickness, in my break-ups, in my grieving, in my financial challenges, in all people, in sadness and joy—and I am still here stronger than ever despite it all. God is everywhere, in everything, and in everyone. It's only a matter of allowing yourself to take the time to look, hear, and feel the presence. Some people only recognize God in a limited capacity through religion; mostly in good circumstances, and only as a man with a white beard and robe in physical form trying to overcome evil. Could there be more and beyond this? What do you think?

43.

"God is love. In the presence of love, sin is not real. Therefore, God cannot judge and cannot be feared. It's just all LOVE."

It just made sense to me to come up with this quote because loving cannot exist at the same time as fear and judgment. Sin cannot exist as it contradicts God's reason for creating mankind. We were not created in God's image and likeness just to be called sinners and to be judged in the end. This is a form of travesty and separation to me, a story created to instill fear and to lose self confidence because of the label "sinner." The

God I know is not even close to this. We have an "unconditional" loving God, right?

44.

"If you have allowed yourself to be taught that you were born out of sin, then it's about time that you also allow yourself to be taught that you were born out of love."

As I was browsing social media, I came across an Atheist page and a Christian page. Evidently, they're opposed to each other. But one thing that motivated me to write this quote was the common thing that these two belief systems have; they both allowed themselves to believe and not believe. Can we then be flexible to accept and reject what still works and what does not for ourselves? It's neither right nor wrong, it's what works for you and what serves your purpose.

45.

"You cannot simply put everything on God and then blame Him when you don't get what you want. In case you have forgotten, you were given free will. You are a co-creator, you have God's DNA, and you are a source of love and peace."

Without the knowledge of my true self as a co-creator to God, I would still be dependent and just waiting and whining when things wouldn't turn out the way I wanted. I am not saying don't turn to or trust God. But I realized that I have the power to create my reality as I am a partner to God and that God and I are one and not separate entities. God has already created the Universe and the rest were already my creation. Therefore, the blame can no longer be on God.

46.

"And you believe and say that you are children of God and that the Creator has and is an unconditional love, so be the Gods and Goddesses you are, born out of love and not out of sin."

This quote is to remind and motivate myself and others of the power, talents, and gifts we have. We are not just ordinary people on this planet. Yes, we believe in God. We say it, and yet it does not manifest in our actions and in our lives. Still, the lack of self-confidence, self-sabotage, self-destruction, anxiousness and loneliness are present. So, are you being a God or a Goddess of power and love?

47.

"God as love created us out of love. Therefore, we were born out of love and not out of sin. We are not sinners but lovers. Rejoice! Celebrate life! Be love."

It's just ridiculous to know that even if we came from love, we grew up being labeled as sinners afterward. This is one of the reasons some people cannot express and do what they really want to do—because of the belief that sinners do not deserve to be happy and celebrate life. I find it very contradictory. God is love and that everything was made out of love.

48.

"God has no needs. God created everything."

I wrote this realizing that I was given information passed on from one generation to the next without me having to think for myself about what and who to believe. I grew up having an understanding and a concept that I have a God needy of praises and worship and who loves me and gets mad if I disobey. I realized that I was barely scratching the surface of my knowledge about God. I have formed a concept of a God who is just like us, in need of attention and who gets disappointed and frustrated. I was so limited. God has no ego to be satisfied. God is all. What kind of God do you have?

CHAPTER FOUR

Quotes about
Separation Beliefs

49.

"The deadliest creation of humans on this planet is not weapons of destruction but separation beliefs."

The condition and state of our entire planet led me to write this quote. We were influenced and taught by society that we are different from each other through gender, race, talent, skill, income status, culture, and religion. If there were greater awareness of us being ONE, there would be no chaos, war, injustice, fighting for human rights, fighting for lives, fighting for the hungry and displaced people, and most especially fighting for peace. There would be no more businesses capitalizing on people's health, country leaders challenging each other, the deadly competitions we have created to find out who the strongest, the fittest, the most beautiful, the most intelligent, the best in different categories just as long as we identify who is more special. This no longer works! Why not start working together building each other up for unity?

50.

"No labels, no separation. It's that simple."

In my early 20's, I realized that because of the rules, standards, classifications, categories and most of all labels which we humans have set for ourselves, we have created more separation. We have a habit of labeling that leads to isolation and separation. We have formed words to label people in terms of looks, intelligence, capabilities, financial status, race, and gender, to name a few. This labeling has tremendous effects that we all witness today. Can we all just be humans living in peace and respecting one another?

51.

"You cannot judge. Period."

Judgment is a way for the ego to be satisfied. When we judge we make the other person wrong in order for us to look and feel right and more entitled than the other. We judge and criticize because we do not have a full knowledge of ourselves, and it is easier to just come up with a conclusion rather than to think first and empathize. We cannot judge another person, as we do not understand what the other person is going through. Every person has a story to tell.

52.

"Stop hating yourself in and through others. We are one."

The bickering, disagreements and endless trying to be right is just absurd. From the media to day-to-day life, I have experienced all these and keep witnessing more. Hating on people indicates a feeling of lack in one's self. Your hating on others is a manifestation of your dissatisfaction with yourself. Realize that we are made complete and all we need to do is share our completeness and enjoy each other.

53.

"When there is unhappiness and dissatisfaction in oneself, judgment is present."

I've had my share of passing on judgment and being judged. I have learned and realized that the only reason we pass judgment is because we are not content with ourselves.

54.

"Anything or any thought that condemns, judges, hates, separates and excludes is not of God."

Love is our true nature. As we all come from love, our words and actions should be the manifestation of our true nature. How are we treating each other?

55.

"Envy and jealousy are such poison to you. They blind and prevent you from experiencing the beauty in life and in others. Try love and acceptance instead."

In this ego driven society, the attention and focus of some is to compete with others on things like status symbols, job title prestige, power, the acquisition of material things, having more money for the purpose of flaunting and bragging a self-image that is better and more entitled than others. Competition, the unhealthy kind, breeds envy and jealousy. If you are only motivated by envy, your relationship with others and yourself is affected. If there were more realization and acknowledgment of self-love and acceptance, envy and jealousy would have no place in this world.

56.

"Failure is imminent unless peace is achieved amongst divided people."

We are ego driven and divided by our beliefs despite the efforts we put in. Hunger and racial discrimination is still a problem. Human rights and global warming are still an issue. The poor get poorer. There are diseases that remain uncured despite innovations in science and technology. We are infinite beings, boundless and powerful co-creators with God. What are we doing with these gifts? Sadly, until now, world peace still seems to be unachievable.

CHAPTER FIVE

Quotes of Hope

57.

"In sadness, I uplifted others, I gained happiness."

I realize I feel much happier when I'm encouraging, empowering and boosting someone's confidence. It's hard to find words to describe it but think of it like eating a moist chocolate cake every time. It's a delightful experience to give a part of you in order to make someone happy. Truly, to give is better than to receive. This is how this quote came about. And I am doing it again at this moment for you.

58.

"Even before a need arises, an answer has already been provided."

In our world of contrast, when there's a problem, there's always a corresponding solution. One cannot exist without the other. As I reflect on my life, I can honestly say that all the questions and problems that I faced before have all been answered and solved. This is how abundant our world is. There is no lack. You just have to believe that it is there, find it and allow it to work in your life. During the process, you might think that it's not available, but it is my friend. Faith in your God and in yourself is strongly encouraged. The Universe is always working for you and not against you.

59.

"It is always bleak for the fearful and bright for the hopeful."

My inspiration for writing this was the election. After every election, people's initial reaction is fear. Because of this fear, protests and rallies form to express resistance and release the feeling of fear. Uncertainty follows fear and eventually results in more separation. When there is resistance, expect more persistence. Being hopeful for the best gives people the chance to believe, work together and build a better nation instead.

60.

"Another day. Another chance. Another opportunity."

I remember dreading each day going to work. I did not enjoy working with a micro manager. I wrote these words on a sticky note and posted it on my computer to remind me that I am blessed and given another day. It's a gift and I just have to enjoy it. Another day, another dollar, I even added. Eventually, it worked.

61.

"Joy: you have it. You were born from it. Feel it, protect it, guard it, and own it. No one can steal it unless you allow them to."

I found myself feeling an unexplainable joy despite the difficulties of my life. I was crying, then laughing, then eventually smiling. No, I was not going crazy. It was a feeling of stillness, a light feeling of peace, happiness, and gratefulness, which eventually helped me to be stronger and face each day with a new attitude. Joy made me appreciate life more. It has always been within me and I just took it for granted. I will never lose this again. I learned more of this from reading inspirational books and listening to the spiritual teachers, authors, motivational speakers, and influencers such as Eckhart Tolle, Deepak Chopra, Dr. Wayne Dyer, Abraham Hicks, Stuart Wilde, Neale Donald Walsch, Bob Proctor, Louise Hay, Barbara Hubbard and so much more.

62.

"Failure is hope to start anew."

Failure in my family was a sign of weakness. I have witnessed my father fail and it took a toll on him. He became irritable, impatient and just angry. Growing up, the expectation at home was too high for us to get good grades. From being a consistent honor student during grade school to not being in the top of my class in high school or college, that was an ego depleting experience for me. I realized that it was just a chance for me to start again, re-create myself and become better. And so I excelled in other things, like directing and writing scripts for plays during college and case study presentations in grad school. Failure is just redirecting your path. It is full of hope and an exciting opportunity. So, time to emerge again, my friend.

63.

"Everything heals.
Today is the day!"

I wrote this in full belief and gratitude, having survived my illness, grief, and other challenges in life. Healing is the next inevitable step in a person's evolution process. I have experienced it and am absolutely sure that you will too. It's a matter of believing and allowing yourself to experience it now. It is always available.

64.

"The beauty of life is that we were given free will to change and create new chapters as many times as we want and anytime we want. You don't like your story? Then change it."

I was able to change my story by recognizing my mistakes first, then accepting and acknowledging my situation and lastly, changing the way I think. All things are possible. I use my free will to create more happiness and peace in my life. One of the ways I do this is by sharing my experiences and lessons learned from past difficulties through this book. Do you like your current life story? How about your chapters? Do you need to go back to the drawing board?

65.

"B-1 is a vitamin that is good for happiness, peace, friendship and love. I advise you to take this every day."

If you want happiness, peace, friends, and love in your life then BE ONE.

66.

*"You can never run
out of positive thoughts.
Never. Because your nature
is love, peace and joy just
like the Creator."*

I realized that had I chosen to think negatively, I would not be able to share my experiences with you. This book would not have been possible. My life would not have changed. The source within our inner being is rich and abundant in love and always working for us, showing us the endless possibilities of positivity.

67.

"A better version of you resulted from you embracing change, allowing yourself to grow and openly welcome criticism. Keep on keeping on."

Many despise criticism because it hurts their ego while others take it as an opportunity to improve. They do not take it personally. Criticisms are like humps on the road that allow you to slow down and assess yourself. People who welcome criticism can easily embrace change. Change is good.

68.

"Everything has been perfectly created. It all depends on how you see and feel it."

We sometimes have a tendency to overreact, especially in difficult situations. This limits our ability to see and experience the bigger picture. We get stuck sometimes seeing just one angle of a problem (and no solution in sight) without realizing that nothing happens by accident. The Universe is always working for our good and always redirecting our path, acting like our GPS, so we can be right where we're supposed to in terms of prosperity, abundance, success, healing, joy, peace, and love. Our planet

Earth was created before us humans were and it can definitely survive without us. It continues to provide oxygen for us to breathe, food for all sentient beings, and a place where we can all co-exist. Isn't this perfect?

CHAPTER SIX

Quotes to Think About

69.

"You make your own Heaven. You make your own Hell. And these are not places to go to."

I had a realization that heaven and hell were just ideas created for people to have a choice about their experience. I believe that where we are right now is heaven. Hell is when we allow ourselves to experience pain, discomfort and stress of any kind.

70.

"There are so many things to be grateful for, once you start you'll find more."

I grew up in an environment where there were only a few expressions of gratitude and mostly complaints. Since the bankruptcy of my father's business, it was a daily habit of each family member to be in a state of lack. We had spoken of lack and acted on lack. We allowed anxiety and stress into the family and our focus was on the things that we did not have. We have forgotten about the most important thing and that was being grateful for having each other. I strive to improve myself. I met beautiful people who eventually became friends and more than family. Their lives became my inspiration. Their love and acceptance of me taught me to be grateful. My perspectives changed. Now, I have been practicing gratitude in everything. I noticed that the more I do this, the happier I become. What are you grateful for today?

71.

"You cannot change people; you can only accept and love them as they are."

Everyone is going through a different path and journey. Everyone has his own level of awareness. Instead of trying to persuade and change a person, start by understanding them . . . know their story. Change starts from within us.

72.

"Let me be,
said the Dream.

Knock, knock,
said Opportunity.

Come back tomorrow,
said you.

I want to soar,
said the Dream.

Open the door,
said Opportunity.

I'm not ready,
said you.

Let's find someone else,
Dream said to
Opportunity."

As evolving creatures, we continue to create, which is one of the purposes of being humans. Some people grab every opportunity that comes their way while some are afraid to leave their comfort zone, making excuses to not embrace change. These excuses are usually the things we tell ourselves stemming from all the negative thoughts we entertain every day. I have made excuses for myself too. I allowed myself to be dictated and influenced by these negative thoughts, which resulted in my dreams remaining just that . . . dreams. When the opportunity to write came "knocking" on my door, I was hesitant at first. But then I realized if not now, then when? Excuses are but an obstacle in your evolution. Once you realize this, you allow yourself to create a better version of your world. Keep the dreams coming and grab all the opportunities you can find, as they are there to help you flourish.

73.

"When we say that we are not perfect, we are saying that our Creator is not perfect. Stop and change this thought habit."

We have been taught this for so long and we have been programmed to think that we are sinners from birth and that we are not perfect. The effect of this on humanity is so great that we have forgotten our true selves and our true nature. The beliefs of the collective consciousness that we are sinners brought more sinners to the world. We cannot live this way, constantly belittling ourselves. We are such powerful spiritual beings. The best example of a person who was able to demonstrate our powers was Jesus Christ. I used him as an example because of my religious background as a Catholic and Christian. He walked on water, healed the sick, raised people from the dead, and he understood and believed what he was capable of. If we were taught to believe that, then how can we not believe that we too are capable of achieving these feats, as we are not different from him. Some may read this and call it blasphemy, but this is something to be realized. People have been living unconsciously and just following whatever they have been told because of the comfort of not thinking at all. It is time to believe and start being the perfect people we are.

74.

"Change in a nation is an opportunity to unite and progress."

It was election time in 2016 here in America when I wrote this quote. History is just repeating itself. When there is change there is reaction. It is just up to us people to decide if we will allow this change to unite us or continue to separate us. Separation beliefs do not work but only add more pain, difficulty, and misunderstanding amongst each other.

75.

**"The thought said: Kill!
But the heart said: No!
And thought said:
Think again!"**

A single thought causes one to speak and act. Our body is designed just to do and without a thought, it would not know what to do or say. Our thoughts initiate everything. What are your thoughts right now?

76.

"People watch, people see, people hear and people feel your energy and vibe more than your words. Make sure they are positive ones."

One sunny afternoon, my husband and I went for a long drive. While in traffic waiting for the green light, the pickup truck next to us started honking. We were wondering why, as there were neither cars passing nor pedestrians crossing. The driver started waving at us. I rolled down my window, the driver smiled and said "that" (pointing to our intertwined hands on the gear), "is just the way to live!" He sped off as the light turned green. My husband and I looked at each other and smiled. We had inspired someone that day. The manifestation of our love could be seen, heard, and felt in what we did and said. My husband and I did not know that just by holding hands, we could inspire someone.

That night after having dinner out, a lady witnessed my husband opening the car door for me in the parking lot. Before closing the door, we heard her say, "Now that's the way to treat a lady . . . You just made me have second thoughts about my man." We drove off laughing. People do really watch. We can change and inspire a person's life for better or for worse both consciously and unconsciously.

77.

"How lovely it is that we can live in this world of contrast and still agree. Some call it friendship."

I know two people who before becoming my good friends, had a misunderstanding. That was decades ago. Friendships can blossom from an ugly foundation, anywhere and anytime. Remember, all of us start off as strangers. What happens next is up to us.

78.

"There are endless opportunities to make someone happy and feel important, and it begins this very moment."

As we always say, life is short, so let us not waste a second without doing something good for people. Always show your appreciation to your friends and loved ones. Never miss an opportunity to compliment someone. If you want to live happier, share your happiness. Go ahead and reach out to people.

79.

"TODAY is always much better than yesterday."

I always find today more exciting and refreshing than the day before. Today gives me new hope, another chance to appreciate, improve and create. How are you today?

80.

"Your number one
attacker comes from
the quality of your own
thoughts, and not from
others. Change them,
you change your
perspectives."

As we generate thousands of thoughts per day, we have a chance to choose which ones consume us and which ones to ignore. Sadly, most of the time we tend to focus on the negative ones and we're often unaware that we are already consumed by them. If regularly done, this can become a habit . . . a habit of being paranoid. I have experienced being in this state of mind at some stage of my life and it's exhausting. I allowed myself to change by renewing my mindset, and it's liberating. I see things differently now. My perspectives have changed for the better.

81.

"You choose what you believe in and live through what you have chosen. The only one responsible in your life is you. Stop putting the blame on others."

I always tell my husband that I do not have regrets in the decisions that I made or blame anyone for what has happened in my life. Without those past life events, I would not be where I am supposed to be today. I was the only person who allowed myself to go through such events. No one forced me and I did not force anyone else to be involved. I wrote and created that life story and now I am writing a new one. I am a co-creator with free will.

82.

"Your beliefs will either make you or break you. Choose them wisely."

What I have and where I am now is the result of the beliefs I have allowed myself to operate from. My family's health history is more on cancer, diabetes, and heart problems. They say it's hereditary, but my views of not believing in this "hereditary" crap freed me from having such diseases. Just because some of my family members had it does not mean I will have it too. I believe that it really depends on how you take care of your body. Instead of allowing myself to be another one of the family statistics, I changed my thinking and lifestyle. Every year, my annual physical exam results can attest to this.

83.

"Every day you have a choice to observe or to judge."

I have always been an observant person. I know that it is better to be this way than to judge people right away. Not that I did not judge before, but as much as I can, my initial reaction is always to observe first as it gives me time to understand things and people better. This leads to acceptance. Instead of passing on judgment or spreading unsolicited opinions, observe and understand the situation. So what are you choosing right at this moment?

84.

P – Preparing you for
A – All
T – Timely
I – Incidents of
E – Excitement and
N – Never ending
C – Chances in the
E – End

Patience is a virtue. Enough said.

85.

"Positivity in everything requires a lot of believing too."

It is important to genuinely believe the positive words that we say to ourselves and to others. Otherwise, it will just be a bunch of words uttered into the air. It is like agreeing but not being fully convinced. Everything should be aligned with our beliefs. This is one of the reasons why some of our dreams do not materialize. When I was diagnosed with aplastic anemia, every cell and fiber of my body did not believe it. Instead, I believed the opposite. I kept telling myself and my body that I was well and that my body would heal me from this sickness. And so after almost four years, I was released by my doctors and have been well ever since.

86.

"Nothing hurts or disappoints when you don't expect."

I have been disappointed many times in the past, especially by people I am close to. I realized that it's because I have set a standard for myself that whatever I did to someone would be done to me in return. I came to accept that people couldn't always be on the same level of standards I have set for myself. And so I changed my standards to not expect from others at all. This change eased me from frustration and disappointments.

87.

"Fewer words, fewer mistakes, less trouble and less drama."

In a discussion or argument, there will be an obvious competition of inflated egos where the goal is to be the one who is right. Growing up in an environment of endless bickering, disagreements, and verbal abuse within my family led to a lot of drama. Many hurtful words were said that could not be taken back. No one wanted to keep quiet. But the damage has been done as they say. To keep quiet in an argument takes a lot of discipline. I learned this further from my husband. He is a man of few words and is always cool, calm, and gentle. His life is simple and thus, less complicated.

88.

"You will always find beauty in every situation. Every situation leads to your destination."

Every life situation has their lessons. Not all situations will be good. Remember that even the worst situations will have their lessons as well. In my lowest times and in the ugliest situations in my life, I found my power in forgiving, compassion, patience, and understanding. No matter what the situation is, allow yourself to find its lesson, its real meaning, and its purpose. The Universe is always working for you and never against you.

89.

S – Something
M – Meaningful
I – In your
L – Life
E – Expressed

Smiling is the most acceptable and the easiest universal language. Everyone understands a smile. It is our way to express ourselves without words. A genuine smile eases feelings of pain and brings us to a state of bliss. Others smile to show approval, some to show their sincerest emotion and for some, it is their habit to smile at everything that comes their way. As the saying goes, it takes more muscles to frown than it does to smile, so don't waste too much energy frowning. You wouldn't want those ugly wrinkles, would you?

90.

"There's nowhere that you can be except in the now. So where are you now?"

I've been guilty of thinking about the future too much and all it brought me was anxiety, worry, and more worries. I remember investing in many retirement plans when I was young, but I just ended up closing them all before their maturity date to meet a present need. I was in a hurry to retire. There was too much planning without considering the present. There is nothing wrong with investing and securing yourself, especially for your retirement, but do not forget to consider your present. I also dwelt so much in the past that all I did was compare. Until I realized that we only have the present moment, the past is already gone and the future is not even guaranteed. Everything is happening nowhere else but in the present moment.

91.

"You will be what you choose to be."

Whatever you choose to think and believe will come to fruition. Our thoughts become things. As the Law of Correspondence states, the world you live in is a reflection of your inner thoughts. You are bound to experience what you think and believe.

92.

"Truth is sweet in the end, bitter at first and sour at the middle."

When my mother admitted to the family that she had a favorite amongst her children, I did not even react nor did I feel any jealousy. At a young age, I was surprised at having no reaction.

Perhaps it's because I already knew. I took it well and handled it maturely I suppose. When I confronted my father about telling me the truth about his sickness, I felt sad and relieved afterward. When I confronted an ex about having another party in our relationship and was told the truth, I felt hurt but later on, I felt free. When it was my turn to tell an ex that I had to end our relationship, I felt free again. The experience of being told the truth and telling the truth is liberating and sweet as it releases me from pain, rejuvenates my soul, and improves my health. It helps me move on with my life.

93.

"To believe is to see."

The old axiom would say the opposite of this quote. My experience inspired me to write it this way. Why is it so? Have you ever dreamed, imagined, and visualized something that it felt so real? So real that you can almost feel it? The person I am today is the person I have imagined and believed myself to be—at peace, happier, healthier, contented, a coach and an author. I have been seeing and experiencing through having a repetitive and consistent thought of what I wanted to become. What I am now is just the manifestation of my past thoughts. I am currently visualizing and believing something else at this very moment and that is you holding my book, reading intently; ready to change for the best.

94.

F – Fixed

O–Outcome of your

C – Centered and

U – Undivided

S – Self

The New Year inspired me to come up with this quote. At the start of each year, people are so pumped up to set a goal but sometimes they lose concentration along the way. When we start to pay attention and fully focus there is no room for doubt. Believe in yourselves and you will achieve great things. So go ahead, FOCUS my friend.

95.

"Everyone wants to be validated, recognized, accepted, respected, understood and loved. But not everyone wants to validate, recognize, accept, respect, understand and love."

The current treatment of people towards one another is summarized in this quote. It's all because everyone is on different levels of awareness of validation, recognition, acceptance, respect, understanding and love that these things are present. It may seem unfair, but this is how it is as every person is operating and living according to his own beliefs and experiences.

96.

"Surrender is the acceptance of what is and the welcoming of evolution."

I have noticed that when we continue to resist things that we do not want, the more those things will persist in our lives. When we surrender and allow ourselves to change, we become more open and receptive. We overpower fear; we become awakened and eventually evolve. If you feel trapped, it is time to surrender and accept now.

97.

"A truly happy and grateful person sees the beauty in everything."

Have you noticed that when you have accomplished something and are just happy and excited about it, you either want to jump for joy, scream, hug someone and nothing bothers you in that moment? Why? It is because you are just filled with positive feelings. And when we fill our lives with positivity and gratitude, we will see even more beauty.

98.

"To be consumed by too many negative emotions is like stopping yourself from living and evolving. Let go. Heal."

Many people have unconsciously programmed their minds and trained themselves to dwell on negativity. Drowning in these negativities, they attract sickness, stress, anxiety, and they become less and less appreciative of themselves and their lives. Their thinking is limited which costs them their growth and improvement. Nothing works and serves their purpose and misery is their company. Time to change this habit. Time to let go. Live and heal today.

99.

"Life becomes much easier with more appreciation rather than expectation."

Gratitude + contentment + acceptance = a peaceful life.

100.

"Good and bad things only happen when you call them forth and allow them to manifest."

Nothing happens without our permission. We have a choice to think either happy or sad thoughts. Our beliefs come from our consistent thinking of a single thought. We live according to our beliefs. Drama, for example, would not just happen and show up if we did not attract it. The thoughts we have entertained and have focused on from the past had something to do with its manifestation in the present. Thoughts become things. Haven't you noticed that when you think of a painful experience from the past and you keep talking about it, more painful experiences appear? Like attracts like. It's the Law of Attraction.

101.

"Love is all, open, naked, endless, boundless and limitless."

Love accepts all without conditions. It is free. No hidden agendas, restrictions, expectations, and judgments.

102.

"It's better to create with your feelings than to react to them."

One of the best lessons I embraced is to always find the beauty in every situation and create something out of it. When confronted by an undesirable situation, let it flow for acceptance. Find the root cause to realize the lesson, and understand the message that the situation is trying to convey. Create something significant out of it.

When we react to a negative situation, joy, peace and the chance to "see the brighter side of things" so to speak, is lost. From my experience, once I have settled down from my initial reaction to the situation, I become more aware of it and start seeing the bigger picture. Awareness brings me to a better understanding, which inspires and motivates me to be creative. This creativity will lead me to cook a new recipe, learn a new hobby, or write a new quote. This is the reason this book became possible. I am living my life as a co-creator with God, a bringer of light, peace, and love. What are you creating right now?

URGENT PLEA!

Kindly leave me a REVIEW of my book on Amazon.

Let me know what you have learned and gained from it. I read each and every review. This way, it helps the book to be more useful to others.

Thank you so much!!!

ACKNOWLEDGEMENTS

I am thankful to God for inspiring me to write this book. I am grateful for my life experiences and lessons learned, as I was able to share them with others.

And most of all, I am thankful to my husband who challenged me with his questions and helped me to improve this book.

I would also like to express my gratitude to my editor, formatter, and designer for taking this book to another level.

And lastly, to my incredible launch team, you all rock!

ABOUT THE AUTHOR

Elsa Mendoza is a Certified Community Life Coach who has a passion for uplifting, empowering, encouraging, motivating, inspiring and helping others to find their passion in life. She helps people identify their strengths and potentials, and rewire their thinking for a better life and relationship to self and others. She believes in the power of positivity and the laws of the universe. Her motivation in doing so is her survival from a harsh family environment during her childhood until her early 20's and overcoming a rare disease that almost took her life. Elsa is well-traveled, has lived in three countries and has interacted with several nationalities, been exposed to different lifestyles, cultures and religions, and has seen what humanity has to offer, thus her inspirations for writing this book.

Elsa holds a Masters Degree in International Business where she has helped small companies thrive by coaching owners on operations and sales development. In her free time, she volunteers at Long Beach Rescue Mission, PAWS LA and Meals On Wheels. Like most of us, she enjoys reading, watching concerts, and traveling with her husband. You can find out more about her at www.changecreateevolve.com.

SELF-PUBLISHING SCHOOL

NOW IT'S YOUR TURN

Discover the EXACT 3-step blueprint you need to become a bestselling author in 3 months.

Self-Publishing School helped me, and now I want them to help you with this FREE WEBINAR!

Even if you're busy, bad at writing, or don't know where to start, you CAN write a bestseller and build your best life.

With tools and experience across a variety of niches and professions, Self-Publishing School is the only resource you need to take your book to the finish line!

DON'T WAIT

Watch this FREE WEBINAR now, and Say "YES" to becoming a bestseller:

https://xe172.isrefer.com/go/sps4fta-vts/bookbrosinc2859

Made in the USA
Lexington, KY
27 February 2018